Our Town

A View of Life in a Small Town and Beyond

– Tim Nimigan –

ISBN: 978-0-9936026-0-3

Book design by Erin Wattam
www.erinwattamdesign.com

Preface

To be from around here, you need to have 'three in the ground.'

I love living in a small town! 'Our Town' of Napanee (now Greater Napanee), has been an especially nice small town in which to work, play, raise a family, and run into people I know anytime I'm walking down the street.

It's taken almost forty years to get to know that many people, but don't let that fool you into thinking I'm 'from around here.' One of my teaching colleagues, Wayne Goodyer, once informed me that here in the heart of United Empire Loyalist country, to be from around here, you need to have 'three in the ground,' meaning, three generations of my family would need to be buried in a local cemetery. So, after a mere forty years, I'm still not 'from around here.'

It's true I was raised a big city boy in Toronto, better known as 'Trawna' to us Torontonians, who by the way, only need to have 'one in the ground.' Nevertheless, I believe my forty years in Napanee have given me some kind of credentials to comment on the culture, customs, flavour, foibles, idiosyncrasies, and generally humorous aspects of living in a small town and rural community. Cartoons seemed to be the perfect vehicle for delivering those comments.

If you think you see yourself in any of the cartoons, may I remind you that most characters appearing in these works are fictitious. Any resemblance to real persons, living or dead, is purely intentional. I trust you will see me as laughing *with you* and not *at you*. Undoubtedly I'm looking in a mirror with several of the cartoons. I must confess, there are a few that have come dangerously close to being full-blown editorial cartoons but I assure you there was never any intent to lambaste anybody. Did I mention, I love being *permitted to live* in a small town?

Preface

As an artist, I'm often asked about a piece of artwork, "How long did it take you?" As a cartoonist, I'm more often asked, "Where do you get all your ideas from?" and, "Do you ever get stuck for an idea?" Most ideas derive from simple observation mixed with a slightly warped sense of humour, an ability to laugh at oneself and a determination not to take some things in life more seriously than they deserve. My wife, Debbie, as well as daughters, Laura and Kayla, have all gotten me kick-started with an idea, in whole or in part, by times. They have also assisted with this book by offering comments written beside some of the cartoons designed to give the reader insight into the process of inspiration. Extended family and friends, too numerous to mention (not to mention they would all want a free book), have also contributed ideas. Sometimes when the idea well has run dry, I have just hopped into the car and driven around town or countryside keeping my eyes open for possibilities. Seldom have I been disappointed.

Lastly, while they haven't had direct involvement in the production of these cartoons, I should acknowledge the undoubted influence in my formative years of a couple of humourists in my family. When I was growing up there was always much laughter at gatherings of the Nimigan clan, if I can use a Scottish term to describe a bunch of Romanians. I'm sure a poll of the family would produce consensus that my Uncle Mark and brother Wayne were the root cause of more than their share of that laughter.

Tim Nimigan

If you enjoy the cartoons, please tell a friend about this book and press "Like."

Foreword

Tim does a fantastic job of encapsulating the little foibles of life in a small, rural town.

When Tim Nimigan approached me about 10 years ago to propose sketching a cartoon for our editorial page, I jumped at the chance. I've always believed that a cartoon always makes an op-ed page better.

Of course, it couldn't just be any cartoon. The cartoon had to fit the audience and the publication. While searing political cartoons are great, that wasn't what I was looking for in *The Beaver*. I wanted something lighthearted, and something that reflected the character of this community.

I don't recall whether or not I gave Tim much, if any, direction in this regard, but what he came up with in those first few weeks was exactly what I was looking for — and exactly what our op/ed page had been missing.

Tim's work — whether it produces a slight chuckle or a belly laugh — always gives me something else: an undeniable sense of familiarity. If you live in Napanee, you are going to see something reflected from your day-to-day life in Tim's cartoons, without fail. Tim does a fantastic job of encapsulating the little foibles of life in a small, rural town. That's why, week after week, it never fails to put a smile on my face.

That's also why I'm sure the cartoons contained in this book will put a smile on your face, too.

Seth DuChene

Managing Editor, *The Napanee Beaver*

My daughter, Kayla, always wanted a dog; I did not. While drawing my first cartoon for "Our Town" (see cover), my concession was to include a dog in all of my cartoons for her sake.

With the second cartoon I started hiding my other daughter's name, Laura, in every cartoon. You might have a hard time finding it in this one since it is in code on the licence plate of the car based on the position of the letters in the alphabet. i.e. 12=L; 1=A; 21=U; 18=R; 1=A. The rest of the cartoons have her actual name somewhere. (Tim)

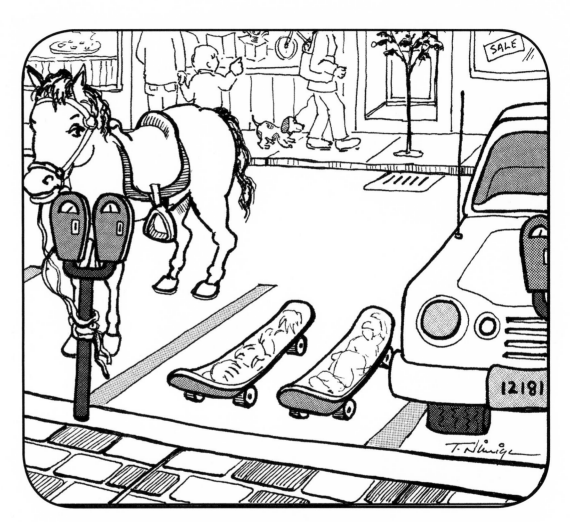

The Mayor calls a meeting of town & country to iron out differences.

"... the heavenly host saying... On earth peace, good will toward men."

This is the first cartoon Tim received a call about. A shopkeeper thought he was encouraging people to do their shopping out of town. It really was a comment about how fickle we can all be with our convictions, even the one to shop locally. (Debbie)

"Next year we tell the fellas they don't have to do all of their shopping in town."

"I'm all for free parking over the holiday season, but I have concerns about the cost of that many bags over the meters."

"It looks like the minister's back from his conference in the big city."

"Hazel, I think there's more than just the coffee brewing."

Since Dad taught at the local high school, he was able to observe many different styles and fashions including all the different ways a ball cap could be worn. Sometimes it just depended on the 'group' to which a student belonged or who was influencing him. (Laura)

How many pizza places does a small town need? At the time of this cartoon we had seven places that sold pizza and there have been three more move in since then. Being as their pizzas are all slightly different, when our family orders pizza we quite often order from more than one place to keep everybody happy. (Laura)

"Apparently it's owned by the same guy who has the all-you-can-eat buffet across town."

"He was saying they sold their bungalow in Toronto, decided to move to a small town and scale down."

One of Tim's first introductions to the slower pace of small town living came when he had to rush downtown at lunch break to pick up some plaster for his afternoon art class. Graham VanSickle was almost finished waiting on Tim when another customer came in and commented on a rainbow outside. Graham responded, "I don't think I've ever seen a rainbow in January. We'd better go and see that." Off he went leaving Tim standing. Tim decided the only thing to do was to join them. Graham always enjoyed hearing Tim recount that story years later. (Debbie)

"In like a lamb, out like a lion, they say, so I don't think we've seen the end of winter yet, do you?"

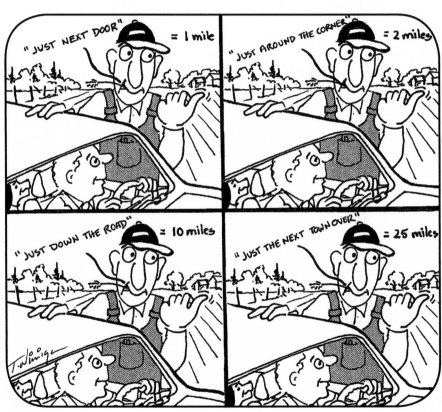

Country Equations

This came after one of our discussions about how many people are likely to be at Dad's funeral and how we aren't going to know at least half of them. (Kayla)

Visit people when they are well so they can really appreciate it. (Tim)

"...and you remember Ethel and her boy Jimmy. Ethel is a neighbour of that friend of your second cousin Mary, that we met in Myrtle Beach that one year."

"Now, that scares me!!"

"I don't really know what it is. It was interesting and going cheap, so I bought it at a yard sale."

We know several people who have shown cattle at the local fair and they taught us that the judge looks for a nice straight back. To make a calf's back appear straighter than it might actually be, the owner will trim the hair straight across. Obviously these kids went a little too far with their attempt at deception. (Laura)

"I hope you're right about this judge being as blind as the one from last year."

In a community where many people have their own gardens, it's no secret that zucchinis grow rampant. People don't want to throw their excess away but finding willing takers can be difficult. (Debbie)

"No! I want one of those!"

"Are you sure you don't want some zucchinis with that?!"

The first year in our house in a subdivision, we were shocked by the number of trick-or-treaters that came to our door just because we were in a 'better location'. Kayla and I knew that if we wanted really generous treats we had to go to the country. Those people 'treated' us really well since they didn't have as many kids through and tended to fill up our pillow cases faster. (Laura)

"So, how do you like living in town?"

"Yes, I do see your point, but moose, walleye, deer and duck, aren't the four we discussed in class."

"Ten bucks says you've got turkey & lettuce!"

"What was that about the back roads being safer than the freeway?"

"If you want more next year, you have to go to where the parade starts and then come down here."

When Laura was three years old we were so proud of her as she began her bedtime prayer close to Christmas, "Thank you that Jesus came to save us at Christmas." Then she added, "…and thank you that Santa knows when we are good and bad." So much for teaching her the true meaning of Christmas. (Debbie)

"Do you think we need to up our Christmas decoration budget next year?"

"I know it's a rush order, but can you tell Santa that those were lies that my brother Bobbie told about me, at the mall today."

"Please say you're kidding.
Today's the 14th right??!!!"

"Everybody knows that if the boot gets knocked
over it's not a goal. I thought I told you that."

I'm sure this is usually just a case of bad timing on the part of us poor shovelers but it makes you wonder. (Tim)

"I didn't want to go by until you'd finished."

"Hey honey, what do you say we both sign up for Hospice's 'Dump The Plump' again this year?"

"

Winter 2004-2005 was an "unusual" one. People in Napanee say that about every year. We missed an event one day because we spent three hours shoveling our driveway. Meanwhile, friends 15 minutes north of us, hardly had any snow and accused us of making up an excuse for not going to the event. (Debbie)

"Yah, we had that stuff yesterday."

When I was little I would wake up around 6 a.m. on Saturday mornings so I could go yard sale-ing with dad. The night before we would look up the 'good sounding' yard sales in the newspaper and determine our plan of attack. It was a pretty special thing for me growing up. (Laura)

"Personally, I don't go by the groundhog. When Pete finally packs it in, I know spring is the very next day."

"Ladies and gentlemen, let the yard sale season begin!"

"Say, do you fellas have that stuff in green?
I'd like to have you come by in July
and do my lawn."

Avid golfers can hardly wait for the course to firm up enough to be opened in the spring of each year but most do wait. These fellows are poster material for impatience. (Tim)

"I think we're the only ones on the course, so it must be yours."

Work Load Ratios

"Just think! Only 364 days until my next day off."

"You say your father only lived here for forty years. Ah! So you folk aren't from around here then."

After Tim retired he enjoyed sending entertaining absentee notes to Kayla's teachers. One time he included a copy of this cartoon. (Debbie)

Some of my colleagues looked forward to my girls being away so they could get the next note ...at least that was the reason they gave me. (Tim)

"I think this is just a classic case of scholastic fatigue syndrome. Call me if you don't see a difference by the end of the month."

In 2003 we went to a beach in California with some of my Grandma's relatives from Oklahoma. Uncle Raymond, a hardcore farmer, decided to wear his Osh-Kosh overalls to the beach complete with a distinctive farmer's tan. (Kayla)

"I always bring my fold-up chair. You just never know when you're gong to get stuck behind one of those Eeee-bayers."

"Do you get down here very often?"

After Tim and I were married, we had a vegetable garden and no end of trouble with raccoons & porcupines eating our corn. Our neighbour told Tim he should keep a radio on out in the garden overnight and it would keep the animals away. Because of the threat of rain one night, Tim covered the radio with his beloved musical instrument, a washtub bass. In the morning we discovered not only had our corn been eaten but also the broom handle on the washtub had been chewed. (Debbie)

"Why do we have to go already? We just got here, and I didn't get to pet the rabbit again, and you promised!!"

"He may be a bit shy, so would you like me to come back and check on him at recess?"

Gas prices were skyrocketing. In the USA gas is priced by the gallon, so gas station signs showed three digits. In Canada gas is priced by the litre so only two digits were needed. That led to some interesting solutions when a third digit became necessary. A good gust of wind and the gas price could drop dramatically. (Laura)

"Hey boss, how much longer do I have to stay up here and hold this?"

"We give thanks for your protection through
these perilous times."

"I'm applying for greeter! How about you folk?"

"Hey Willy, isn't that your Uncle Bob?!!"

Whenever anyone starts to dig a big hole in the ground, rumours immediately circulate about which store or restaurant is coming to town. Over the years, if I had a dollar for every time I've been told a Swiss Chalet is going to be built, I'd be rich enough to buy the franchise myself. (Laura)

Note: This cartoon was published in November of 2005 and finally in 2013 there is a sign soliciting a franchisee for a Swiss Chalet to be built out near the 401. Could it really be?

"This is nothing compared to what we used to get. Why when I was a kid we used to have to..."

"Don't worry! I read about this idea in the book I got for Christmas called, *Snowmobiling For Dummies.*"

After Tim retired he'd go to the coffee shop in the morning even though he doesn't like coffee. Here are a couple of local auctioneers, Tom Harrison and Neil Lambert with Jace Godfrey. Hartsel Martin, who found a six finger mistake in a previously published cartoon, got his name on the back of the truck outside. (Debbie)

"Oh, I dunno. What are you fellas gonna do today?"

What makes someone famous or well known? One could rise to stardom and be famous worldwide because of a musical talent as in the case of Napanee's Avril Lavigne. Then there are the Harold Flanagans (Pepsi-Cola Petes) of this world who quietly weave their way into the fabric of a small community and leave a big hole when they are gone. Our Harold was arguably just as well known in our community as Avril. Those who picked him up when he was hitchhiking to an auction or social gathering knew him to be a gentleman and a man of faith. (Tim)

"I don't know who she's supposed to be but, hey, there's Harold! Wave everybody!"

Any resemblance to Chris Seeley (left) in this cartoon is purely intentional, I assure you. (Tim)

This is a pretty good interpretation of what Chris and Dad look like, only Dad does not carry weights and never wears a headband, and rightfully so. (Laura)

"I know it's just been three days, but I think I already feel a difference in my energy level. How about you?"

"We just have much more than we need."   "Can you believe the bargains in there?!!"

"I'm pretty sure that's not what the folks had in mind when they hoped you'd make your mark in this world."

This must be Dad. When Mom asks him to go shopping, he often has trouble figuring out exactly what brand, what type, or what size she had in mind. If you look down the list you will see the trouble is only getting started with the Cheerios. After the original version of this was published, one person, Hartsel Martin, called to ask Dad if there was any significance to the man having six fingers. Dad had forgotten the finger up to the man's mouth counted as one. (Laura)

There are at least two other cartoons in this collection with the same six finger mistake which Debbie found while proofing. I left them "as is" for you to have fun finding. (Tim)

"... and especially thanks that mom couldn't remember where she put the can of Lima beans."

"I couldn't find mine."

PC stood for President's Choice long before it stood for Political Correctness (don't get me started). I'll let the cartoon speak for itself beyond that. (Tim)

"Blabbermouth!!"

"I like your balanced approach but aren't you afraid of offending your neighbours with that?"

I sometimes look down our street on Halloween to see if there's a chartered bus sitting there. Actually, it is fun to see all the costume ideas. One year when I asked a very young Laura what she wanted to be for Halloween, she said "An Oreo Cookie". Not wanting to disappoint an intent little girl, I carved the two biscuits out of styrofoam, painted them dark brown, and created a sandwich board that she wore over white clothes with white boots, white hat, white scarf and painted white face. (Tim)

"No, my parents aren't with me. I'm not flying anywhere. I was just wondering if you could help me with something."

"The law might say you had the right of way, but local custom says we take turns at this intersection."

This should be a picture of Mom. When she taught kindergarten she would get so excited about snow days. In winter her favourite TV show was the weather. If it looked like school could be cancelled the next day, Mom would get up in the night to check the weather channel and look out the window. (Laura)

"Hi, is this the radio station? This is the guy from the bus company that cancels the school buses."

I'm guessing Dad, being a friendly guy, has been guilty of posing this question in this circumstance on more than one occasion. (Laura)

"Hey, hi everybody! How y'all doin'?!"

"I must say, your old bath towel for a tablecloth and going all out for the Hungryman's are a nice touch."

"I've always thought it was important to try and relate to my grandchildren."

Bill and Marion are going on a Caribbean cruise with their refund. Where do you think we could go?"

Our house in Newburgh was the first one on the left just past the "Happy Halloween" bridge. Vandals with spray paint were responsible for the name. After the graffiti wore off, the locals continued to refer to it as the "Happy Halloween" bridge much to the puzzlement of newcomers and visitors. (Debbie)

"You need to turn around and go back down here a ways; turn right where Jed's garage used to be; go past Silas Peckham's cow pasture; under the Happy Halloween bridge, and it's somewhere in there. You can't miss it."

"I can't get to your yard sale tomorrow, so do you mind if I come in and try to rip you off tonight instead?"

"Not bad, mind you last year I caught five at least this long off this very same dock."

I feel like we've had this type of conversation on more than one occasion. Dad usually starts it and Mom has the final word. (Laura)

"... but think of all the money we could save not having to stay in motels!"

"So is there some medical law that says the weight you lose can't come from the same place you put it on?"

"So, are you looking forward to the holidays, Bobbie?"

"So if I've never had a garden here before, I'd like to know who told the tomato worms that I planted one this year?"

"So here's the deal. You don't kill me and I won't tell your teachers the real reason you're not in school this week."

"I trust we've all had a relaxing and refreshing summer, are excited to be back and ready to focus on the challenges ahead."

Tim has always enjoyed camping. For the most part I don't mind it. However, I don't particularly enjoy walks to the shower house, planning and preparing meals in small spaces, dealing with mosquitoes, listening to noisy neighbours, walking into wet towels hanging inside the trailer when it rains, taking the last campsite available due to a motorcycle rally in town … (Debbie)

"The guy in the office said they've had a cancellation and we can stay for two more nights. What do you think?!"

During an election campaign the electors try to determine if there are substantive differences among candidates. Pictures of these four local candidates in the newspaper suggested there was at least a difference in 'style'. The caption is a quote from an old laundry detergent commercial. (Tim)

"Would you like any...?"

I can see the difference.
Can you see the difference?

"Well sweetie, I think we just discovered the
origin of the phrase, 'Brace yourself!'"

"Whoever needs to be dropped off first,
get in the van last. Next year you're all
taking swimming."

When I finally convinced my dad to get a dog, he asked if he could stop putting one in each cartoon since we had the real deal. I told him that Laura had her name her whole life and he still put it in the cartoons so the dog had to stay. He did change the type of dog from this point on to resemble Keita. (Kayla)

"Something tells me we need to just see this as a donation."

"Before you say no, can't you just imagine how much fun it would be to have a puppy?"

59

"It's okay. She just said keep your *feet* out
of the water."

"I know you need to go outside Toby, but
you'll just have to wait until we have
finished sorting out the recycling."

In 2007, Christmas displays that Dad and another Art teacher had been asked to make years earlier made their annual appearance on the lawn of the Memorial Building. Santa with his toys, sleigh and reindeer, as well as a snowman, stack of gifts, Mary, Joseph, sheep and donkey were all set up. Conspicuously absent was the baby Jesus, probably lost in storage and apparently deemed unnecessary. A 'miracle' occurred on Christmas Eve when a cardboard baby in a manger mysteriously showed up, painted in a style remarkably similar to that of the other pieces. It rained several times during the next week but the cardboard baby Jesus looked as fresh as it did the night it was put up by 'someone.' (Laura)

"Look mommy! It's just like in the story!
There's no room for Jesus."

"I'm thinkin' my chances might be better here than the last few places I tried."

In 2008 Premier Dalton McGuinty's government instituted Family Day in Ontario to take place on the third Monday of every February. This seemed like an idea too good to be true. (Debbie)

"Didn't I tell you there'd be a catch?!"

"Just a little off the sides."

"It seemed like a good hiding spot at the time."

"Isn't spring such a beautiful time of year?!"

Tim came proudly home from an auction with a handy car polisher that only cost him $5. In thirty years of marriage, I believe Tim has only polished the car once or twice when we first got married. I'm sure this gadget will be the motivation he needs to do it more often but no signs of that yet. (Debbie)

"Let's see if I can guess. You've been to another auction. You've found the handiest thing and I won't believe how little it cost."

"You have to admire their determination,
year after year."

"He says *thrifty*. I say *cheap*."

I know faith and optimism are good things but when it comes to new festivals and events, why not wait until the second or third year before announcing it as an annual event, just in case? (Laura)

"So, how's it going so far?"

"Hot enough for ya?"

"Be a dear and count that for me will you sweetie?"

"Uh-uh! You have to at least wait
until the fair is over."

"Well you can just tell your candidate,
I'm not impressed!"

Locker clean-out days were held twice a semester at our high school and always produced some interesting aromas I'm sure were not the type used by aroma therapists. Gym clothes and old lunches were the usual culprits. (Tim)

"This year, try not to have the school calling the police to check out your locker with cadaver dogs again."

FIRST BAPTIST CHURCH
THIS WEEK'S SERMON
"THE FIRST SHALL BE LAST
THE LAST SHALL BE FIRST"
MT. 19:30

"How long do you think it will be before they catch on that neither one of us is letting anybody through?"

Our friend Judy Wilde inspired the idea for this cartoon after telling us about seeing a construction crew at work in front of her dentist's office. Tim changed the setting so it was in front of our own dentist's office. He got quite a kick out of it. (Debbie)

"Any chance you could do that after business hours? We've had an unusually high number of cancellations today for some reason."

At one point the Napanee Beaver announced there would be some changes to the format as well as the distribution schedule of their newspaper. This poor fellow demonstrates how imaginations can run away with us and how rumours get started. (Tim)

"What's this I hear about you people making changes to the beaver?!"

"I can't imagine your elves are any too happy about all the outsourcing you seem to be doing to China these days."

"Nice touch! Did it take you long to come up with the list?"

When yet another pharmacy chain announced it was coming to town to add to the several that were already here, I came up with this tongue-in-cheek idea for putting our town on the map. If they aren't careful, pharmacies are going to give the number of pizza places a run for their money. (Tim)

"You're so subtle!"

"I really don't mind the cold. How about you?"

"It's really easy Grandpa. All you have to do is..."

Once again, Chris Seeley, Tim's walking buddy, appears in a cartoon. Chris asked Tim if he could look after their two cats while he and Rosaleen were away for the weekend. Out of a desire to help, Tim said yes but if truth be known, he really has no room in his heart for cats. (Debbie)

Would you believe, you we're the only one of our friends who wasn't busy this weekend?"

The U.S. government's financial bailout of some giant auto manufacturers dominated the news at the time of this cartoon. (Tim)

"But Grandpa, I thought you said you could use a bale out."

"Do you mind if I open it and check before you ring it through?"

"It's OK sweetie. I had Poppy help me in the garden for 10 minutes this morning and now he's working on an Oscar."

Have you ever noticed how some people just seem to have the scoop on everything that is going on around town? Dad's friend Chris seems to be one of those people so imagine the concern that it caused when Chris announced he would be moving to Cobourg. Fortunately, he came back. (Debbie)

"It's not the loss of a walking partner and the exercise that your move has me worried. I'm just wondering how I'll get in on all the rumours about what's going on around town."

"She apparently said something to the clerk about them being for her grandmother's 100th and then just vanished into thin air."

"This happens to me whenever I open the garage door on a Saturday. NO, I'm not having a sale!"

Does it strike anybody else besides me as funny that a hospital has what is called a 'privacy policy?' Sure, I understand it on one level, but there are so many other levels. (Tim)

"Chances are you probably do know a lot of other patients in here but I'm afraid I can't be showing you the list due to our privacy policy."

"May I just say ladies, that your internet advertising and signs out at the highway are a little misleading."

"Friend or foe, Mom?!!"

"You can stop anytime now. I think
we got the message!"

"The nice chap in the pro shop said you guys
were short one for a foursome and probably
wouldn't mind me joining you for a round."

In 2009, an oddity occurred in the school year calendar. The first three days of school came on the Tuesday to Thursday prior to the Labour Day weekend instead of beginning on the day after Labour Day Monday. It led to a bit of a staggered start as not all parents and students bought into the idea. (Tim)

"I don't know how other parents are handling it, but I feel like I'm playing 'Deal Or No Deal' with Jimmy. He says if I don't make him go until after Labour Day, he'll skip three fewer days this year to make up for it."

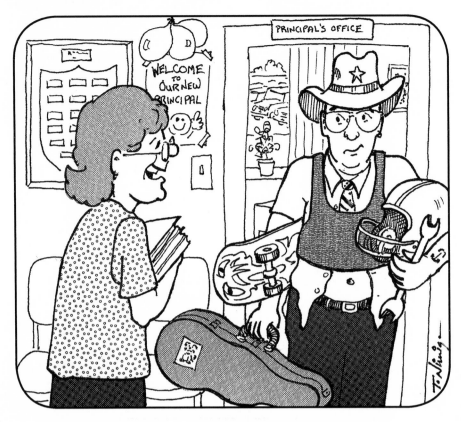

"I see you've been to the
'Making Connections' seminar."

One of the fundraising sales in which Laura and Kayla were obligated to participate was the sale of chocolate. We found it was less stressful to buy all the chocolate and eat it than to try and sell it. (Debbie)

"Look Mommy! I can see the word 'FUN'.
Can you see it?"

"This one has a very nice verse."

"Apparently people are not encountering any
construction if they go this way. We're
going to fix that today."

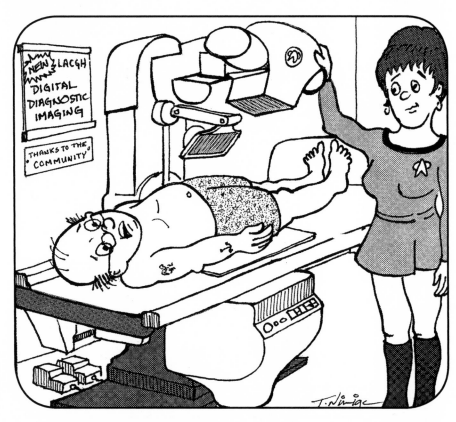

"So with the new equipment, am I still getting 'X-Ray'ted?"

The Post 9/11 era saw increased border security which meant all Canadians had to produce a passport when crossing into the USA whereas before ID such as a driver's licence had been sufficient. Nets cast wide often catch the unintended. (Tim)

"You can tell your boss we're not at all happy about the new regulations."

When grandma moved to Napanee, we saw that peer pressure is not just a problem for young impressionable teenagers. Only in this case, instead of competing for the most advanced mobile device, it was the best mobility device. (Laura)

"You must be the new lady from room 306."

"We have an opportunity to go to Florida for 6 months beginning next Tuesday. Do you think that will have any impact on Jimmy's mark?"

"Don't worry. I'm sure it doesn't mean anything."

"I'm going to talk to the manager. It's not right
that you should have to push that up there
without some kind of snow tires!"

I feel sorry for God in certain types of situations where He must be caught between a rock and a hard place. Then I remember it's more important that we please Him than that He pleases all of us. (Tim)

"So, do you think our prayers are just cancelling each other out?"

"He wants to know if the organizers had considered having a mascot for the week."

87

Reading the real estate pages can be more humorous than reading the comics. Just think of the words "real" and "estate" for starters. Then read between the lines as you read the descriptions. Not only that, have you ever seen a $250,000 house advertised as costing "a quarter of a million dollars." (Debbie)

"What about this one?! It says it's affordable, a handyman special, just needs some TLC, our own personal touch can be added to the unfinished basement, very private with view of lake, and on top of that, it's the feature home!"

"Your idea was brilliant! Grandma's gone from not doing any of the exercises the doctor prescribed to not missing a day in the past month."

"Well, as the sign clearly says, sir, you get a half chicken and they are not on sale, just on special."

"See! What did I tell ya? No way you shoulda been charged for skatin' here yesterday. The sign says it's FREE! I'd be fightin' it dude."

"It's his Spring version of a New Year's resolution. It always lasts two or three days or until hockey playoffs start—whichever comes first."

My grandma is quite the fashionista with lots of outfits and accessories to go with those outfits. When most women stopped wearing hats to church, she was one of the last holdouts. She finally did concede and didn't always wear one, but that didn't mean she was willing to get rid of any of them. (Kayla)

"So, do you think I should call the paper and cancel the yard sale ad?"

"Am I missing something? You say you need to Facebook your friends to keep them up to date with what's happening, but all you ever seem to do is Facebook your friends?"

"I'm home!"

In 2010 the 8% federal sales tax (GST) and 5% provincial sales tax (PST) were rolled into one harmonized sales tax (HST) which was set at 13% and touted as better for the consumer. You do the math. (Tim)

"It's not working for me, how about you?"

"Okay, ...so what if I said I'm working my
way through college?"

"Don't worry. I'm sure they will get along just fine."

Mom and Dad had their work in lots of art shows. When they got home from a show, we would ask them how it went. If they said, "It was good exposure," we knew they hadn't sold anything. (Kayla)

"How are sales going so far?"

It can be tough to make a decision between candidates in a small community. I suppose if we made them based on the candidates' positions on the issues it would help. (Tim)

"... because one's my old moose hunting buddy, one's my wife's nephew, one's my neighbour, one's my barber's brother-in-law, and one fella's wife looked after our dog while we were away."

"No, Mom. I mean the new boy in our class, he came from Toronto. Where did I come from?"

"Yes I remember what the doctor said. Did you notice I cut back on gravy on my second helping and I'm only having one piece of pie?"

"I didn't know you've been going to the denturist! I could have told you about getting these for a fraction of the cost at the dollar store."

People in a small community take their church suppers seriously and there are plenty of them available. We don't always go to them but whenever we do, some of the same people are at every one. I often wonder if there's any point to these folks having a stove in their house. (Tim)

"Will you help me look for my bag of Halloween candy?"

"Do you remember when we would do this for the Beatles concerts and Leaf playoff tickets?"

"It's your brother. He wants to know how the bathroom reno is going and whether we want Christmas at their place or ours."

"Do you happen to know what this means?"

"I told him if he was planning on buying me a
sweater again, he'd know he had the right size
if he just tried it on upside down."

"That was really fun Grandpa! Can we come back after lunch?"

"My wife says, based on my symptoms and her computer, I have all of the diseases on that list. I'm here to get a second opinion."

Ken and Ronda Williams, Robert and Joshua, would invite us over for their Friday night special of homemade hamburger and fries from time to time. They were gooooood! Over time we came to realize that we were probably seeing the full extent of Ken's taste in food. Here he is with his sidekick, Gary. (Tim)

"Go ahead and use Wiarton Willie and robin sightings if you want. Personally, I go by Motorcycle Mike."

"Any chance your 'culinary artist' could whip us up a burger with fries and gravy?"

This cartoon is a little trip down memory lane. I remember dad taking me all over town to find different materials so I could test their thermal conductivity. The results convinced Dad to use an aluminum cookie sheet whenever he needs to defrost frozen meat. (Laura)

Thanks, Rob. (Tim)

"Mom, do you know where the pop bottle went that I was using for my science experiment?"

"I don't think my mom is very happy about the mark you gave me on her science fair project."

"The internet is great! I found it on
www.reversibleumbrellas.com."

"Buying a memory foam mattress at an auction
wasn't a good idea. It's still remembering the
previous owners."

"Don't worry! All the other girls in our cabin have been here before. I'm sure they will be glad to show you around and make you feel welcome."

"No, I'm sorry. We don't have a washroom on board."

Citing a safety issue, a school bus driver was told Christmas decorations were not allowed on school buses. However, it seemed suspiciously like part of a larger plan that already included not having any Christmas decorations inside the schools lest they "offend" somebody. Okay, so I admit, this cartoon got a little political. Don't get me started. (Tim)

"We use the Shepherds for bomb and drug detail, but it's these little fellas you want when it comes to finding Christmas decorations.

105

Some great ideas, theories and philosophies have been battered, bruised or rendered ineffective when attempts have been made to put them into practice in the real world. (Tim)

As Tim and I drive on country roads, we often comment on how solar panels, intended to protect the environment, take away from the beauty of the environment. I wonder if these huge solar panels will be in landfill sites someday, right beside the old monstrous satellite dishes? (Debbie)

"I wasn't interested either. Then this company came along with the only system developed to blend in with the rural landscape."

"How about one gold filling for one fill up and we call it even?"

107

"I'll say it was a bad break, and just when I
seemed to be getting a head!"

"My dad says I gotta get a job.
Ya' got anything?"

If any of you met my dad when you were getting close to that significant moment of elementary school graduation, three pieces of advice you likely received for the next step, that of high school, were:

1. Choose your friends wisely;
2. Be careful who you hang around with; and
3. Choose your friends wisely. (Laura)

"Hey look Mom! I think Goldie has learned a new trick."

On St. Patrick's Day even people who aren't Irish go to great lengths to claim Irish decent. Saying, "Hannigan, Flanagan, Milligan, Nimigan," usually works for me. The sound of our name worked for my mom too when she started dating my dad and her father asked her if 'Nimigan' was Irish. She said, "Something like that." She knew full well it would have been a short courtship if he'd found out it was an anglicized Romanian name. (Tim)

"What part of Ireland did you say the O'Lanterns were from?"

One evening I came home from a kitchen party hosted by a friend. As I was explaining to Tim how the party worked and how much money I had spent, I could tell the cartoon inspiration levels were on the rise. (Debbie)

"If you order over $999 worth of tools tonight, your host, Tony, will receive a unique ergonomically designed sewer snake."

"Bob and Nancy forgot to send us an invite to their New Year's Eve party tonight. They want us to go over now. What do you think?"

"Marilyn called. Jim just bought a 110".
Apparently the guys want to have the
Super Bowl party there now."

"Don't worry, mister. Just put them under your
pillow tonight and you'll get some money."

"I think the reason people retire is so they'll have enough time to go to all their medical appointments."

"I said SWEEP! not TWEET!"

"I know just *exactly* how you feel."

"Never mind reducing the waiting times for
medical appointments—do something about them
at the Tim Horton's around the corner."

Did you notice anything about the house in the background? Dad usually limited shading to areas of intended focus. Our neighbours inspired this exception when they modernized by painting their front and garage doors two different colours, clearly underestimating how much conversation it would spark. (Laura)

"... not until Billy's dad raises his allowance and promises never to ground him again!"

"Nothing personal, I assure you. I just think I need to go back to my original plan."

"I know young people can think their grandparents are old and out of it, but we've still got a good idea or two, buster."

"Just think! By not buying bags, not only did you help the environment, you just saved twenty-five cents."

"What would you charge to take me to my car just past the reserved parking?"

"Is anybody ready to make a guess?"

This is just one of a lot of funny stories our friend, Judy Wilde, tells about things that have happened to her. I'm sure the same thing has happened to lots of people but I think Judy is the only one who enjoys admitting it. (Kayla)

"There's something wrong with your pumps. I've driven around them three times now and they are still on the wrong side of my tank."

"So what do you think? Did I pass?"

"Hey, mister. Is your dog friendly?"

"Ever since he retired from teaching, the sights of a passing school bus seems to get him all some kind of emotional."

When our youth pastor and his wife, Dusty and Krista Crozier, had their second little girl, Kaitlyn, she was born with a full head of black hair that stood straight up and out. It was extremely cute and obviously too much of a temptation for this cartoonist. (Tim)

"It looks like our old dog has been teaching new tricks."

"I'm wondering if you have any old stock of pre-litigation ladders."

"Apparently the overnight hike in the price of gas was due to frost damage done to the apple blossoms last spring."

"Me and my brother have started a volunteer organization to help people get rid of their left over candy. You got any?"

"... and would you describe yours as a small, medium, or large car?"

I enjoy noting the names of businesses. In the course of my extensive research into this topic, I've come to the following conclusion. If a business name includes the word "Modern," the owners would be wise to set aside a certain percentage of their intake for ongoing upkeep of their facility. (Tim)

"Altogether now...BIG finish...watch me!"

"Oh Dad! You're so dramatic. You say we never really talk anymore, but what do you think we're doing right now?"

"From what I've been able to ascertain, the noise seems to be coming from the watchamacallit rubbing against the thingamajig. You know what I mean?"

Sometimes cartoons are inspired by a conversation with friends. I asked my friend, Margaret Landry, if she had eaten at a certain restaurant and how it was. She said she had eaten there and then added, "Let's just say their suggestion box is so full you can't fit in another comment." (Debbie)

"Bye, bye now. How was everything tonight?"

"When I was a kid, we had to sing 'a cappella'... in a snow storm ... and uphill both ways."

Has this happened to anybody besides me? Don't you just hate that! A pain persists, you make an appointment, you wait for the appointment date, you get into the doctor's office and, as we like to say around here, "There it was…gone." (Tim)

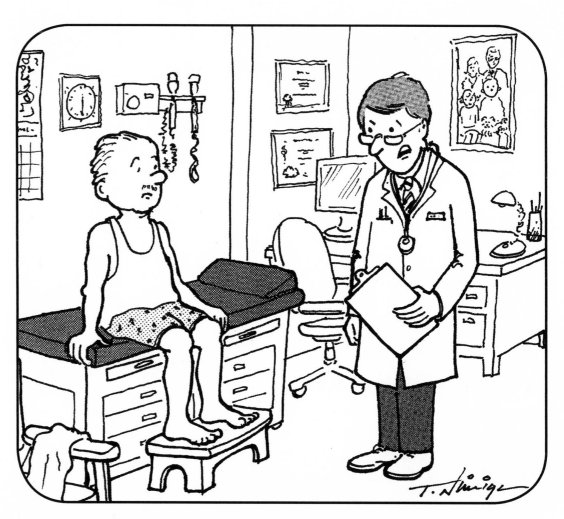

"So, you aren't sure of the location, nature, severity, or frequency of your pain, but you know you had it up until you were coming in from the waiting room. Anything more you can tell me?"

"I trust you realize that by blaming your lack of production on middle age crisis, you now have to live to one hundred and twenty four."

"Are you a friend of the Mack's or the Peecee's?"

"Must you be so dramatic? It was only one day past and besides, that's not what 'Expiry date' means."

My mom was a kindergarten teacher and a thorough planner. We would know ahead of time from conversations at home what the class performance was supposed to be like. There were some similarities between the expectations and reality. (Kayla)

"I'm guessing this is not going exactly according to their teacher's script."

"Show off!"

"It looks that way, but I'm not really over.
Eight are mine, eight are my mom's eight my
daughter's, and eight for the food bank."

"I'm from the Early Childhood Education Council of Canada and want to make sure you are aware of the cutting edge full day Pre-Pre-Pre Readiness programs in your area."

"I'm going down to see the owners of that restaurant we ate at last night. These are about the size they like to serve."

A lot of donation boxes for used clothing have been showing up around towns along the 401 corridor including ours. Some of the boxes are of dubious origin since calls to the phone number on the side of them never resulted in finding answers to what 'charity' people were supporting with their donations. Oh well, at least they inspired this cartoon when I needed one. (Tim)

"Yes, Mom. I did *'happen'* to notice the *'little'* photo of you and dad that you thought I'd like to have at school."

Do you remember my previous comment about checking the newspaper ads for the "good sounding" yard sales? (Laura)

"Please tell me that's not your sign!!"

"I overheard a guy saying these frequent flyers
can be turned into airmiles."

"Do you happen to remember seeing a number
on there somewhere?"

Remember the saying, "Behind every great cartoonist there's a caring, patient, beautiful, intelligent, creative woman." Life with Tim is full of laughs. (Debbie) …and groans. (Kayla)

If you can't find me, I'm on the internet trying to find that saying. (Tim)

"I'll help *again* on one condition. Next time someone's marvelling at how you come up with all your ideas, you let me answer."

Acknowledgements

My family is at the top of my list of acknowledgements. They proved to me that a book was a possibility in 2009 when they presented me with a single copy of a book of the first five years of "Our Town" cartoons that Laura had published on-line. It was definitely an inspiration for getting this one done.

This book wouldn't have been a reality without handing my cartoons over to somebody who could perform their magic and actually make a book out of them. My thanks to Erin Wattam for her graphics expertise, patience, and flexibility as we worked through drafts and rewrites.

Being as I was an art teacher and not an English teacher, I thought it prudent to pass the text portions of this book over to someone who really knows what they are doing when it comes to grammar and punctuation. A former teaching colleague, Janine Murray, was more than equal to the task.

When I needed a current photo of myself for the back cover, I didn't need to hold my camera out at arm's length, take my chances on the lighting and hope I was actually in the frame of the picture. Anita McLarry applied her skills and used excellent equipment to make me look good. I don't understand why that took so long.

Thank you to Jean Morrison and Seth DuChene who felt my cartoons were deserving of being published in *The Napanee Beaver*. I've enjoyed being stopped in the street by many of your readers over the years who would tell me about how a particular cartoon made them smile or laugh.

Then there are all the people who provided me with material for the cartoons. Most of you had no idea you were helping me because, at the time, you were just being you. I hope you don't feel nervous around me in the future. Since cartoons are due Wednesday morning, just stay out of sight on a Tuesday and you should be okay.